W9-BKA-940

Cool
Chinese and Japanese
Cooking

Fun and Tasty Recipes for Kids

Lisa Wagner

TO ADULT HELPERS

You're invited to assist up-and-coming chefs! As children learn to cook, they develop new skills, gain confidence, and make some delicious food. What's more, it's a lot of fun!

Efforts have been made to keep the recipes in this book authentic yet simple. You will notice that some of the recipes are more difficult than others. Be there to help children with these recipes, but encourage them to do as much as they can on their own. Also encourage them to try new foods and experiment with their own ideas. Building creativity into the cooking process encourages children to think like real chefs.

Before getting started, set some ground rules about using the kitchen, cooking tools, and ingredients. Most importantly, adult supervision is a must whenever a child uses the stove, oven, or sharp tools.

So, put on your aprons and stand by. Let your young chefs take the lead. Watch and learn. Taste their creations. Praise their efforts. Enjoy the culinary adventure!

visit us at www.abdopublishing.com

Published by ABDO Publishing Company, a division of ABDO, P.O. Box 398166, Minneapolis, Minnesota 55439. Copyright © 2011 by Abdo Consulting Group, Inc. International copyrights reserved in all countries. No part of this book may be reproduced in any form without written permission from the publisher. Checkerboard Library™ is a trademark and logo of ABDO Publishing Company.

Printed in the United States of America, North Mankato, Minnesota
102010
062013

 PRINTED ON RECYCLED PAPER

Design and Production: Colleen Dolphin, Mighty Media, Inc.
Art Direction: Colleen Dolphin
Series Editor: Liz Salzmann
Food Production: Frankie Tuminelly
Photo Credits: Colleen Dolphin, Photodisc, Shutterstock

The following manufacturers/names appearing in this book are trademarks: Argo®, Arm & Hammer®, Gold Medal®, House Foods®, Kame®, Kikkoman®, Marukan®, McCormick®, Morton®, Pyrex®, Old London®, Roundy's®

Wagner, Lisa, 1958-
   Cool Chinese & Japanese cooking : fun and tasty recipes for kids / Lisa Wagner.
      p. cm. -- (Cool world cooking)
   Includes index.
   ISBN 978-1-61714-659-6
   1. Cooking, Chinese--Juvenile literature. 2. Cooking, Japanese--Juvenile literature. I. Title. II. Title: Cool Chinese and Japanese cooking.
   TX724.5.C5W25 2011
   641.5951--dc22
                          2010022191

Table of Contents

Explore the Foods of China and Japan

Have you tried Chinese or Japanese food? These two countries are very different, but they have some things in common. For example, rice is the main food grown in each country. People there eat rice every day!

China is about the same size as the United States. But it has four times as many people! Almost half of Chinese workers are farmers. Japan is about the same size as California. It is made up of four main islands and many smaller ones. That's why the Japanese eat a lot of fish.

Chinese cooks often use a pan called a wok. Woks are used to cook food quickly over high heat, so vegetables stay brightly colored and crisp. Japanese cooks often use foods that are in season. That's when an ingredient is at its best! Are you ready for a tasty adventure? Put on your aprons and off we go!

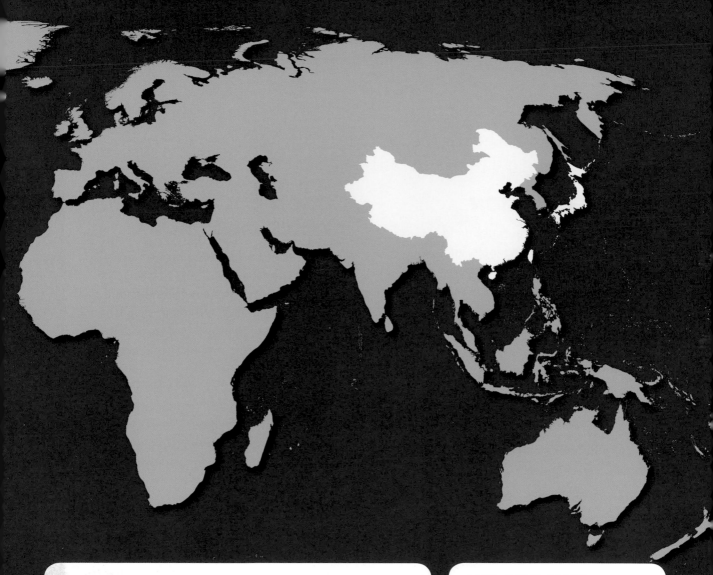

GET THE PICTURE!

When a step number in a recipe has a dotted circle around it, look for the picture that goes with it. The circle around the photo will be the same color as the step number.

4 →

HOW DO YOU SAY THAT?

You may come across some Chinese or Japanese words you've never heard of in this book. Don't worry! There's a pronunciation guide on page 30!

The Basics

Get going in the right direction
with a few important basics!

ASK PERMISSION

Before you cook, get permission to use the kitchen, cooking tools, and ingredients. When you need help, ask. Always get help when you use the stove or oven.

GET ORGANIZED

- Being well organized is a chef's secret ingredient for success!

- Read through the entire recipe before you do anything else.

- Gather all your cooking tools and ingredients.

- Get the ingredients ready. The list of ingredients tells how to prepare each item.

- Put each prepared ingredient into a separate bowl.

- Read the recipe instructions carefully. Do the steps in the order they are listed.

GOOD COOKING TAKES PREP WORK

Many ingredients need preparation before they are used. Look at a recipe's ingredients list. Some ingredients will have words such as chopped, sliced, or grated next to them. These words tell you how to prepare the ingredients.

Give yourself plenty of time and be patient. Always wash vegetables. Rinse them well and pat them dry with a **towel**. Then they won't slip when you cut them. After you prepare each ingredient, put it in a separate prep bowl. Now you're ready!

BE SMART, BE SAFE

- If you use the stove or oven, you need an adult with you.

- Never use the stove or oven if you are home alone.

- Always get an adult to help with the hot jobs, such as frying with oil.

- Have an adult nearby when you are using sharp tools such as knives, peelers, graters, or food processors.

- Always turn pot handles to the back of the stove. This helps prevent accidents and spills.

- Work slowly and carefully. If you get hurt, let an adult know right away!

BE NEAT, BE CLEAN

- Start with clean hands, clean tools, and a clean work surface.

- Tie back long hair so it stays out of the way and out of the food.

- Roll up your sleeves.

- An apron will protect your clothes from spills and splashes.

- Chef hats are **optional**!

KEY SYMBOLS

In this book, you will see some symbols beside the recipes. Here is what they mean.

HOT STUFF!
The recipe requires the use of a stove or oven. You need adult assistance and supervision.

SUPER SHARP!
A sharp tool such as a peeler, knife, or grater is needed. Get an adult to stand by.

NUT ALERT!
Some people can get very sick if they eat nuts. If you are cooking with nuts, let people know!

EVEN COOLER!
This symbol means adventure! Give it a try! Get inspired and invent your own cool ideas.

No Germs Allowed!

Raw eggs and raw meat have bacteria in them. These bacteria are killed when food is cooked. But they can survive out in the open and make you sick! After you handle raw eggs or meat, wash your hands, tools, and work surfaces with soap and water. Keep everything clean!

The Tool Box

A box on the bottom of the first page of each recipe lists the tools you need. When you come across a tool you don't know, turn back to these pages.

SMALL SHARP KNIFE

CUTTING BOARD

HAND MIXER

MEASURING CUPS

MEASURING SPOONS

LIQUID MEASURING CUP

PREP BOWLS

MIXING BOWLS

WOODEN SPOON

PASTRY BRUSH

RUBBER SPATULA

WOODEN SKEWERS

AIR TIGHT CONTAINER

TONGS

FORK

PEELER

PAPER TOWELS

BAKING SHEET

SAUCEPAN

LARGE PLATTER

KITCHEN SCISSORS

STRAINER

POT HOLDERS

LARGE FRYING PAN

WOK

WHISK

HEAVY-BOTTOMED
SAUCEPAN

BLENDER

SLOTTED SPOON

TIMER

WIRE BAKING RACK

Cool Cooking Terms

Here are some basic cooking terms and the actions that go with them. Whenever you need a reminder, just turn back to these pages.

FIRST THINGS FIRST

Always wash fruit and vegetables well. Rinse them under cold water. Pat them dry with a **towel**. Then they won't slip when you cut them.

CHOP

Chop means to cut things into small pieces with a knife.

DICE

Dice means to cut food into small squares about ⅛ inch on all sides.

MARINATE

Marinate means to soak food in a seasoned liquid.

MIX

Mix means to stir ingredients together, usually with a large spoon.

WHISK

Whisk means to beat quickly by hand with a whisk or fork.

SLICE

Slice means to cut food into pieces of the same thickness.

MINCE

Mince means to cut the food into the tiniest possible pieces. Garlic is often minced.

SAUTÉ

Sauté means to fry quickly in a pan using a small amount of oil or butter.

PEEL

Peel means to remove the skin, often with a peeler.

GREASE

Grease means to coat a surface with oil or butter so food doesn't stick.

The Coolest Ingredients

BABY BOK CHOY

YELLOW ONION

SCALLIONS

CARROTS

MUNG BEAN SPROUTS

GINGER ROOT

GARLIC

FROZEN GREEN PEAS

RED PEPPER

CUCUMBER

GREEN PEPPER

BROWN SUGAR

FIRM TOFU

SHORT-GRAIN RICE

SUGAR

GROUND WHITE PEPPER

MUSHROOMS

SESAME SEEDS

SALT

CASHEWS

PEANUTS

ALMONDS

ALL-PURPOSE FLOUR

GROUND CHICKEN

EGG

ANGEL HAIR PASTA

**BONELESS, SKINLESS
CHICKEN BREASTS**

ALMOND EXTRACT

PEANUT BUTTER

LEAN BEEF STEAK

BREAD CRUMBS

SHIRATAKI NOODLES

BUTTER

SESAME OIL

OYSTER SAUCE

Allergy Alert!

Some people have a reaction when they eat certain foods. If you have any allergies, you know what it's all about. An allergic reaction can require emergency **medical** help. Nut allergies can be especially **dangerous**. Before you serve anything made with nuts or peanut oil, ask if anyone has a nut allergy.

RICE VINEGAR

CANOLA OIL

Salt and Pepper to Taste?

Some recipes say to add salt and pepper to taste. This means you should rely on your taste buds. Take a small spoonful of the food and taste it. If it isn't as salty as you like, add a little salt. If it needs more ground pepper, add some. Then mix and taste it again.

MIRIN

SOY SAUCE

CORNSTARCH

BAKING SODA

Chinese and Japanese Extras

Take your Chinese and Japanese cooking to the next level! The ideas on these pages will show you how.

PERFECT PASTA EVERY TIME!

Different kinds of pasta have different cook times. The suggested cooking time is always on the package.

1 Put 4 quarts of water in a heavy-bottomed saucepan. Add 1 tablespoon of salt and stir until it **dissolves**.

2 Bring the water to a boil over high heat. The entire surface of the water should be bubbling. Add the pasta and stir gently.

3 Wait for the water to begin boiling again. Then set the timer for the time shown on the package. Boil the pasta uncovered and stir it every few minutes. Make sure the pasta doesn't stick to the bottom of the pan.

4 Set a strainer in the sink. Pour the pasta into the strainer to drain. Serve immediately with sauce.

STUPENDOUS STEAMED RICE

Makes about 4 to 6 servings

INGREDIENTS
2½ cups short-grain white rice
3 cups cold water

1 Put the rice in a strainer and rinse.

2 Put the rinsed rice and water in a heavy, medium-size saucepan.

3 Bring to a boil over high heat. Cover the pan and turn the heat to medium. After 10 minutes, turn the heat to very low.

4 Cook for another 15 minutes. Do not peek! If you remove the cover the rice will not steam properly.

5 Turn off the heat and let the rice stand for 10 minutes. Before serving, fluff the rice with a fork or rubber spatula.

COOL CUCUMBER SUNOMONO

Makes about 4 to 6 servings

INGREDIENTS

2 tablespoons rice vinegar
2 teaspoons sugar
1 teaspoon water
1 tablespoon soy sauce
2 cucumbers, peeled, seeded and sliced thin
sesame seeds

1 Mix all the ingredients except the cucumbers in a small bowl. Stir until the sugar **dissolves**.

2 Put the cucumbers in a mixing bowl. Pour the sauce over the cucumbers. Stir to mix well.

3 Refrigerate for 1 hour before serving. **Garnish** with sesame seeds.

CHARMING CHINESE GREENS

Makes about 4 to 6 servings

INGREDIENTS

6 baby bok choy, stem end trimmed off
¼ cup oyster sauce
2 teaspoons water
⅛ teaspoon ground white pepper
1 tablespoon canola oil
2 cloves garlic, minced

1 Fill a heavy-bottomed saucepan half full with cold water. Bring the water to a boil over high heat. Carefully add the baby bok choy to the boiling water. After 30 seconds, remove the bok choy. Use a slotted spoon or a strainer with a long handle.

2 Drain the bok choy on paper **towels**. Mix the oyster sauce, water, and ground pepper together in a small bowl.

3 Heat the canola oil in a large frying pan. Add the minced garlic and sauté for 1 minute. Add the oyster sauce mixture. Stir and cook until the mixture is bubbly. Add the bok choy. Stir only until it is coated with the sauce. Serve on a large **platter**.

Sensational Sesame Noodles

These yummy noodles are easy to make and take!

MAKES 4 SERVINGS

INGREDIENTS

8 ounces angel hair pasta
3 tablespoons sesame seeds
¼ cup peanut butter
¼ cup water
3 tablespoons soy sauce
2 tablespoons sesame oil
1 tablespoon brown sugar
1 tablespoon rice vinegar
2 cloves garlic, minced
¼ teaspoon white pepper
2 scallions, chopped
½ red pepper, diced
1 cup fresh mung bean sprouts
¼ cup peanuts, chopped

TOOLS: prep bowls
measuring spoons
measuring cups
small sharp knife

cutting board
heavy-bottomed
 saucepan
strainer

baking sheet
blender
mixing bowl
wooden spoon

timer
pot holders
4 dinner bowls

1 Preheat the oven to 275 degrees. Follow the instructions on page 16 to cook the angel hair pasta.

2 Rinse the cooked pasta with cold water. Stir to separate the strands. Leave it in the strainer to drain.

3 Spread the sesame seeds on a baking sheet. Put them in the oven for 5 minutes. The seeds will turn a light golden brown.

4 Put the peanut butter, water, soy sauce, sesame oil, brown sugar, rice vinegar, garlic, white pepper, and sesame seeds in a blender. Blend until smooth.

5 Put the drained pasta in a large bowl. Pour the blended ingredients over it.

6 Stir gently with a large spoon until the pasta is evenly coated with the dressing. Divide the pasta into four bowls.

7 **Garnish** each bowl with scallions, red pepper, bean sprouts, and peanuts.

Chicken Meatball Yakitori

See why snacks on skewers are so popular in Japan!

MAKES 6 TO 8 SERVINGS

INGREDIENTS

¼ cup mirin

1 tablespoon sugar

½ cup soy sauce

1 pound ground chicken

1 egg yolk

2 teaspoons ginger root, peeled and minced

1 tablespoon soy sauce

½ cup bread crumbs

6 scallions, finely chopped

canola oil

TOOLS:
prep bowls
measuring spoons
measuring cups
small sharp knife

cutting board
small saucepan
wooden spoon
mixing bowls

baking sheet
pastry brush
timer
pot holders

wooden skewers

1 Preheat the oven to 400 degrees.

2 Put the mirin, sugar, and ½ cup soy sauce in a small saucepan. Heat over medium heat, stirring until the sugar **dissolves**. Let the mixture **simmer** for 10 minutes, stirring occasionally. The mixture thickens to syrup as it cooks.

3 Remove the pan from the heat. Pour the mixture into a small bowl. Set it aside. Put all the remaining ingredients except canola oil in a mixing bowl. Mix the ingredients with your hands. Make sure you wash them first!

4 Get your hands wet. Roll small pieces of the meat mixture between your hands to make meatballs. They should be about 1 inch across.

5 Grease a baking sheet with a small amount of canola oil. Put three meatballs on each wooden skewer. Set the skewers on the baking sheet.

6 Bake for 5 minutes. Remove the baking sheet from the oven and turn the skewers over. Make sure you use a pot holder! Bake for 5 more minutes. Take the meatballs out of the oven.

7 Turn oven temperature down to 325 degrees. Brush the meatballs with the sauce. Bake for 3 more minutes to heat the sauce.

Tip

To get just the egg yolk, crack the egg into a small bowl. Use a slotted spoon to gently lift the yolk from the white.

Spectacular Sukiyaki

This fast-cooking Japanese dish is too good to miss!

MAKES 4 TO 6 SERVINGS

INGREDIENTS

1 cup water

½ cup soy sauce

½ cup mirin

2 tablespoons sugar

3 tablespoons canola oil

1 pound lean beef steak, cut into thin strips

1 large yellow onion sliced into moon shapes

3 carrots, peeled and sliced into thin slices on the diagonal

8 mushrooms, cut in half

1 package of shirataki noodles

1 14-ounce package firm tofu, cut into 1-inch cubes

6 scallions, sliced into 1-inch pieces

TOOLS:

prep bowls
measuring spoons
measuring cups
small sharp knife

cutting board
small saucepan
mixing bowls
wooden spoon

large, heavy-bottomed pot
tongs
kitchen scissors

peeler
strainer
timer
pot holders

1. Put the water, soy sauce, mirin, and sugar in a small saucepan. Cook over high heat. Stir with a wooden spoon until the sugar **dissolves**. When the mixture boils, remove it from the heat and let it cool. This is the sauce.

2. Make sure the prepared vegetables are handy. You will need to add them to the pot quickly.

3. Put the canola oil in a large, heavy-bottomed pot. Heat over medium-high heat. Add the beef. Sauté for 2 minutes. Use tongs to turn the meat. Move the meat to one side of the pan.

4. Add the onions and carrots. Keep each ingredient in its own part of the pot. Sauté for 3 minutes. Add the mushrooms.

5. Stir the vegetables to keep them from sticking to the bottom of the pot. Add the sauce and bring to a boil.

6. Drain the shirataki noodles. Put the noodles in a bowl. Cut them into several pieces with clean kitchen scissors. Add the shirataki noodles, tofu, and scallions to the pot.

7. Cook until the meat is no longer pink and the vegetables are hot. The total cooking time should be about 10 minutes.

8. Serve in large bowls with steamed rice on the side.

Even Cooler!

Try using other vegetables such as thinly sliced potatoes, spinach, shitake mushrooms, enoki mushrooms, leeks, or Napa cabbage.

Cashew Chicken Stir Fry

This popular Chinese restaurant dish is even better when you make it at home!

MAKES 4 SERVINGS

INGREDIENTS

2 tablespoons oyster sauce

1 tablespoon soy sauce

⅛ teaspoon ground white pepper

2 teaspoons sesame oil

water

1 boneless skinless chicken breast.

2 tablespoons cornstarch

2 tablespoons canola oil

1 bunch scallions, cut into 1-inch slices

1 green pepper, cleaned and cut into thin strips

6 thin slices peeled ginger root

½ cup cashews

TOOLS: prep bowls
measuring spoons
measuring cups
small sharp knife

cutting board
whisk
paper towels
mixing bowl

wooden spoon
wok or large
frying pan
timer

pot holders

1. Put the oyster sauce, soy sauce, white pepper, 1 teaspoon sesame oil, and ¼ cup water in a mixing bowl. Whisk well.

2. Rinse the chicken and pat it dry using paper **towels**. Cut the chicken into cubes.

3. Put the cornstarch, 2 teaspoons water, and 1 teaspoon sesame oil in a large bowl. Whisk until smooth. Add the chicken pieces. Mix well to coat the chicken. **Marinate** the chicken for 15 minutes.

4. Heat the canola oil in a large frying pan or wok over medium high heat. Use a wooden spoon to remove the chicken from the marinade. Put the chicken in the pan. Sauté for 10 minutes.

5. Add the scallions, green pepper, and ginger. Sauté for 5 minutes.

6. Add the cashews and oyster sauce mixture. Stir to coat all the ingredients with the sauce. Cook for 5 minutes, stirring often. The sauce will thicken a little bit as it cooks. Test one piece of chicken to be sure it is cooked in the middle. If there is no pink color, the chicken is done.

7. Serve over steamed white rice.

Chinese Fried Rice

Leftover rice becomes a delicious meal!

MAKES 6-8 SERVINGS

INGREDIENTS

2 tablespoons canola oil

3 cloves garlic, minced

1 cup frozen green peas

8 mushrooms, sliced

6 cups rice, cooked and cooled

3 tablespoons soy sauce

1/8 teaspoon ground white pepper

5 scallions, chopped

2 eggs, lightly beaten

1 cup mung bean sprouts

TOOLS: prep bowls, measuring spoons, measuring cups, small sharp knife, cutting board, mixing bowl, wooden spoon, wok or large frying pan, timer, pot holders, whisk

1. Heat the canola oil in a wok or a large frying pan. When the oil is hot, add the garlic. Sauté over medium-high heat for 2 minutes.

2. Add the peas and mushrooms. Sauté for 2 minutes. Add the rice and stir well using a wooden spoon.

3. Add in the soy sauce, white pepper, and scallions. Continue to cook and stir for 5 minutes.

4. Make a well in the middle of the rice. Pour the eggs into the well. After about 30 seconds, cover the eggs with the rice. After 1 minute, stir to blend in the eggs.

5. Continue stirring until the eggs are cooked. Add the bean sprouts and stir to mix before serving.

Even Cooler!

Make chicken fried rice! Cut a boneless skinless chicken breast into small cubes. Add the chicken after Step 1. Sauté for 5 minutes before doing Step 2.

Or make **shrimp** fried rice! Use eight cooked, medium shrimp. Remove the shells and tails. Cut the shrimp into small chunks. Add it to the fried rice in Step 2.

Crunchy Almond Cookies

INGREDIENTS

2 cups all-purpose flour

½ teaspoon salt

1 cup sugar

½ teaspoon baking soda

12 tablespoons butter, softened at room temperature

1 egg, slightly beaten

1½ teaspoons almond extract

36 whole almonds

1 egg yolk

2 teaspoons water

Enjoy these sweet treats after a nutritious dinner!

MAKES 3 DOZEN COOKIES

TOOLS:

prep bowls	whisk	wire baking rack	airtight container
measuring spoons	slotted spoon	timer	
measuring cups	pastry brush	pot holders	
mixing bowl	baking sheet	hand mixer	

1 Preheat the oven to 325 degrees. Lightly grease the baking sheet.

2 Stir flour, salt, sugar, and baking soda together in a large bowl. Add softened butter. Mix with a hand mixer until the mixture looks like crumbs. Blend in the beaten egg and almond extract.

3 Wash your hands. Then squish the mixture together until it forms a smooth dough.

4 Roll a small piece of the dough into a 1-inch ball. Put it on the baking sheet. Gently press down with your fingers to flatten it just a little. Repeat this with the rest of the dough. Place the cookies 2 inches apart on the baking sheet.

5 In a small bowl, whisk together the egg yolk and 2 teaspoons water. Use a pastry brush to lightly brush each cookie with the egg mixture. Press an almond in the center of each cookie.

6 Bake for 20 to 24 minutes. The cookies are done when they are lightly golden on top.

7 Remove the cookies from the baking sheet. Set them on a wire baking rack to cool. Store them in an airtight container.

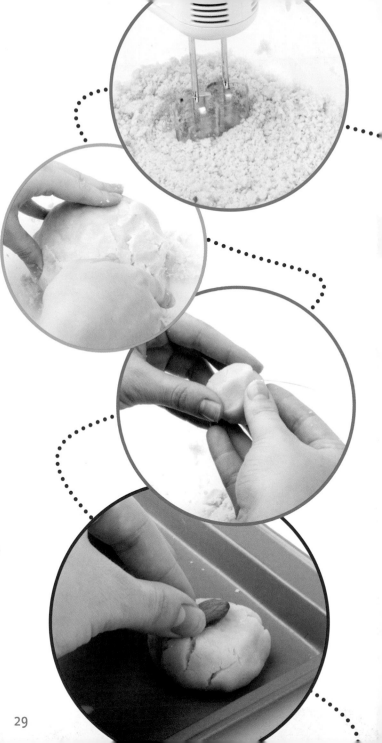

Wrap it Up!

Now you know how to make **delicious** Chinese and Japanese dishes! What did you learn? Did you try any new foods? Learning about recipes from around the world teaches you a lot. You learn about different **cultures**, climates, geography, and tastes.

Making international dishes also teaches you about new languages. Did you learn any new Chinese and Japanese words in this book? These new words will help you sound like a native speaker. You'll be able to use them at restaurants and **grocery stores**.

Chinese
bok choy (bok choi)

wok (wok)

Japanese
mirin (MEE-reen)

shirataki (shee-rah-TAK-kee)

sunomono (soo-noh-MOH-noh)

sukiyaki (soo-kee-YAH-kee)

tofu (TOH-foo)

yakitori (yah-kee-TOH-ree)

Glossary

culture – the behavior, beliefs, art, and other products of a particular group of people.

dangerous – able or likely to cause harm or injury.

delicious – very pleasing to taste or smell.

dissolve – to become part of a liquid.

garnish – to add small amounts of food to finish a dish.

grocery store – a place where you buy food items.

marinade – a sauce that food is soaked in before cooking. To marinate something means to soak it in a marinade.

medical – having to do with doctors or the science of medicine.

optional – something you can choose, but is not required.

platter – a large plate.

shrimp – a small shellfish often caught for food.

simmer – to stew gently at a soft boil.

towel – a cloth or paper used for cleaning or drying.

Web Sites

To learn more about cool cooking, visit ABDO Publishing Company on the World Wide Web at **www.abdopublishing.com.** Web sites about cool cooking are featured on our Book Links page. These links are routinely monitored and updated to provide the most current information available.

Index